Colours of the Moon

New writing from
Artemesia Arts
poetry competition
2023

MOSAÏQUEPRESS

First published in 2023

MOSAÏQUE PRESS
Registered office:
70 Priory Road
Kenilworth, Warwickshire
CV8 1LQ

Cover illustration: *La Mer and Le Ciel* (oil on silk)
Copyright © René Shoemaker 2023

ISBN 978-1-906852-66-5

Foreword

Having put on my judge's wig and gown, I sit and joyfully read through the entries for this, the first Artemesia Poetry Prize. With a wide variety of styles and subject matter, the standard was particularly high, which made whittling down the final selection almost impossible. So many poems, so many difficult choices.

But as poets must write, so judges must judge, and I finally reached a verdict.

My congratulations to the winners and to all the poets who took part. It was a privilege to read your poems, and I feel the wiser for it.

Roger McGough
June 2023

Contents

About the winner...

 Philip Bellamy was "delighted, but very surprised" to find himself the winner of the inaugural Artemesia Arts competition with his poem 'Algorithm'. He says: "At best, I was hoping it might be considered good enough to get into the anthology..."

Philip says he studied creative writing many years ago, where he wrote, in his words, "bad poetry and even worse prose". He lives in retirement on the Fylde Coast in North-West England after a 35-year career working in academic libraries in roles including subject liaison, information literacy teaching and IT support.

Where did 'Algorithm' come from? He says: "Unusually, this poem was ninety per cent inspiration and ten per cent perspiration. Like many, I've been following the recent developments in artificial intelligence (AI). After listening to one of Frank Skinner's excellent poetry podcasts, the idea of reflecting on AI in poetic form came to me suddenly when I thought of the terms 'If... Then' as the start and finish of an algorithm. This gave me the structure and conceptual framework; the stanzas took shape in my mind very quickly, then were re-worked in several drafts.

"This is the first time in many years that I've entered a competition. I'm glad I did!"

Philip Bellamy

Algorithm

What if Erling Haaland had chosen chess
And his only goal
Was to topple a king.

What if Muhammad Ali had become a monk
So he could quietly tend his allotment
And shadow-box with God.

What if Margaret Thatcher had remained a chemist
So she could develop a milk substitute
That suckled infants throughout society.

What if Einstein had merely played the violin
At a seedy hotel in Bern,
Scratching out a living by fiddling tips.

What if Darwin had stayed at home,
Aimlessly watching caterpillars become butterflies
While waiting on his butler to announce lunch.

In the multiverse all this may have happened,
May be happening.
In the confused code of a chatbot it always is.
But here in our overwrought, overthought world,
Where alarms are ringing but go unanswered,
Where everything is instant and celebrity cheap,
Where rolling news cascades into oblivion
And not so smartphones define reality,
The truth is really quite simple.
But then the truth always is.

Bequeath

*On receiving my German passport, courtesy of my Jewish mother's
ancestry. She arrived in England in 1947, having survived WW2.*

The passport comes, *vielen Dank, Mutti,* thin
but history-full, blood-burgundy cover with
eagle, *Reisepass,* no queuing now with Brits

brexited out of the fast lane, their choice.
Mutti: her double helix takes up half my body
and more than half my life; I carry it across

pencil-line borders like an old 78, scratchier
each generation as I pass it down, barcode
boogie and we dance, a wartime coda. When

she chooses to leave I find her in a chipped-paint
hospital room, aneurysm-paralysed, hair still jet
black, so damn beautiful in her lonely dying, no

passport for this, this last border, no ticket
needed, even the poor can travel, nothing to
declare except you tried. Crying is no good;

when it stops all you've lost is water. German
moments bang around my boy-memories and
I open the passport searching for her legacy

and see only myself.

Lizzi Linklater

RUNNER-UP
ARTEMESIA ARTS
POETRY
COMPETITION
2023

Asteria Responds to Pension Talk

While you were sunk happy in the sofa explaining pensions,
a fairy darted from the Pyracantha, passed through the window
and faded in a wisp of red smoke. You'd got to 'options'
when your pottery, (built on Tuesdays in a shed on a moor
someplace), started its revolt. The sleek vase kicked the plump
pot, the clunky bowl hovered, its lip stern.

(When he paused, they resumed their positions.)

At 'lump sum' and 'monthly allowance' the room went crazy.
Cushions spat, art ate itself, candles self-combusted,
the Ficus shrieked like an opera singer with a torn larynx,
and the piano quietly unbuilt itself note by note. But you,
deaf and blind to the hullaballoo,
went   stead   ily   on.

(It was all I could do to feign focus.)

When we could all bear no more, when the bone-weary
house wilted, I conducted an end with the promise
of more pow-wow later. A relieved pastel sky frothed up
an orchestral calm. I gathered my flowing robes
and slipped away, to sit awhile among the stars
before they fell, to enjoy some useful conversation.

*Asteria: Titan goddess of nocturnal oracles
and falling stars in Greek mythology.*

England is a hard place

Bliss in the town, till the next high
rise. There are drugs here, down
alleys, in bankers' creamy toilets;
your job is to ambulance the ODs;
your job is to bless them, father,
for England is a hard place.

In DNA kiosks in the night, under
bleary bulbs on the road to the bridge,
lovers share needles and hindsight
over a map of the forsaken world; we
are nearly America now as the bricks
rot; cry, for England is a hard place.

The child is ill-clothed, ill-fed, and
ill. The child is English, and can prove
it in a test, but the canvas flag is too
heavy and she falls and becomes
foreign. No-one can spell *foreign*, but
it is the worst thing to be, for England
is a hard place.

Lizzi Linklater

HIGHLY
COMMENDED
ARTEMESIA ARTS
POETRY
COMPETITION
2023

11

Air Test on a Building

There's an air test on your building today;
its third. No air must be allowed to sneak in.
It must not sob through cracks. The control
layer has to be impermeable.

Until the air barrier system is tested, pressures
on wind, stack and fan certified, your building
is unusable; a mere collection of corridors,
lift shafts, icy glass walls.

You're stressed. I'm useless.
In our draughty morning bed, I ask,
'Why would it fail?'
'How could it fail?'

You hiss at me,
make more air escape.
I sit tight, dodging spit.
I wish I could uncoil you,

Air must not leak from your building.
It tornadoes from ours. Gales roar,
they judder walls, crash against
door frames, crosswinds collide.

You pray that the air test will pass.
Then you'll come home, survey the rubble,
sigh at the stout weeds, observe the heaved
foundations. Wait for the hurricane.

Bridges and Clocks

I wait on the bridge
I cross the bridge
one way then the other

I look at the clock above the hotel
and I wait on the bridge

cirrus clouds scrape above
the turbid river scours below
people shrug off work for the day
and I wait on the bridge
and I look at the clock

an office group stands below it
drinking in the sunshine
with cold pity in their eyes
as I wait on the bridge

as I wait on the bridge
then see that downriver there is
another bridge
where someone else
crosses back and forth
looking at another clock.

Charlie Mawer

The Bench at Beer

The sign on the bench said;
"In treasured memories
Of a special son and grandson,
Who loved Beer".
We caught the moment
In our collective throats,
Between laughter at the place name,
And the out of natural order tragedy
Of any parent or grandparent
Writing those words.
The clumsiness we felt,
The shingle shifting and reforming,
As the earth reminded us
Of the daily difficulty of
Putting one foot in front of another,
One word in front of another.

Bitter Lemons

Interlocked leaves of two fig trees offer shade.
Retsina, glasses icy with condensation,
revives parched throats. We squint
through sun, eyes unshielded.

Pupils, sharp with concentration,
in corrugated skin, focus unflinching
on backgammon games. Arthritic
fingers lift cups of coffee, treacle-dark,
chink them back into saucers to toss dice,
flash counters, white and black, around the board.
Smiles of triumph reveal other boards
of gaps and crooked teeth.

Intertwined, we stroll along the port.
You buy five kilos of lemons in a net sack,
hoist it onto my shoulder for a photo.
Smiling under my burden I'm unaware
that our love, like too many lemons,
might rot with the weight of neglect.

Steve Stevenson

Ghost Box

Do you remember our thickset
Cathode Ray TV which
long after it was disconnected from the mains,
exuded an unearthly light
washing up against the littoral of the living room
through the dark dead hours?

Once I found our six-year-old standing by that TV,
her cheek pressed tenderly to the screen,
whispering to her dead grandfather.
Static had raised the down of her face
to a microscopic dance,
the fine blonde hair at her nape
crazy with photons.

Bereaved, raw, I whispered
"Dada can't hear you lovely"
and she replied fiercely, incredulously
"I know that!"
as if speaking to a dim child.

The moment fractured.
And never returned.

Now I watch that old tape,
my father seated on the garden step, squinting,
hand shielding his eyes, bemused,
watching his granddaughter play.
All crushed shadows and burnt-out highlights,
image offset,
ghost
of a ghost.

Siberia

Your first physiotherapy session
was tough like the Siberian cold,
making your skin blush like a sun
caught in a spirit bubble of winter sky.

The therapy room felt Victorian,
with a pyramid of dumbbells,
balancing bars, a hall of mirrors,
and two taxidermied donkeys
pretending to be exercise bikes.

You could've sworn the physiotherapists
once worked for P. T. Barnum:
their twiddly moustaches and waves
of chest hair bursting out of their polo
shirts making them ready to tame
invisible lions.

Perhaps you were delirious
from the exercise, imagining grouse,
capercaillies and other animals
in the room: a Siberian tiger.
A mountain range of Bactrian camels.
A Kamchatka brown bear, back arched
like a vaulted ceiling. Red deer. Stoats.

And, inches away from you, a tundra wolf
quietly licking its lips while your penitent
shadow slumped to its knees.

Judith Wozniak

HIGHLY
COMMENDED
ARTEMESIA ARTS
POETRY
COMPETITION
2023

17

Caring for Frida

'Dr Eloesser, my doctor and my best friend'.

She has to sit to work now. Splashes of oil-paint catch
in the folds of fabric in her lap where the easel nestles.
Her speckled funerary beads streaked with brush strokes.

Each time our lives touch I see a different face of Frida.
To others she seems to have mastery over her suffering.
Swathed in shawls she conceals her crushed body

in billowing ground-skimming skirts, voluminous blouses
embellished with embroidery; lapis lazuli hummingbirds,
sunset-orange marigolds. Her gift to me, a self-portrait,

her hair braided with coral bougainvillaea, dark brows
meet like rooks' wings. A thorn necklace pierces her.

Wrong One

You went with the wrong one -
that turned out to be the right one.
If you had gone with the right one,
it would have been the wrong one.
But you didn't. You wouldn't. You couldn't.

There was probably only ever one.
And the rest is language, not even scientific.
For trees don't not grow by volition,
extinct marsupials do not exist,
and empathy emanates from the wrong one.

The right one, who was wrong, holds forth elsewhere,
and the wrong one is your personal truth.
Besides, what is not wrong? Lost love,
the falling of bombs, wedding joys,
the girl found hanging in the bathroom.

Abroad in Thought

Casa Milà, Barcelona

Where the walls curve is movement, my palm rests
On the limestone and electrons dance among themselves.
Had I been more intelligent...or smaller...or just thin

Air

My fingers would've dropped in like carbons,
Rising and falling beneath the balconies.

The architect mouthed *nothing is invented*

These walls arrive from watching waves
And
This house has not yet become. It retreats
And retreats further, back to an origin lying
Somewhere in the ribcage of a
Blue whale.

When I am inside and being digested I see

You

Staying whole, and he explains to me that this is normal.
Here you are a discovery to be left untouched,
Like the walls you have movement, lying in the stillness.

So I notice your arms, the joints angled like branches
Breaking out from the blossom trunk.
Thick green tears sprout from your hands but only fall
As orange flowers, slowed by the thin air.
Thin air holding carbon.

And if I were carbon, I'd fall again.
Disappearing through your wooden rib cage and
Retreating, retreating towards an origin and

Becoming

A Monster's Anatomy

His left foot was from a trainee lion tamer and
though more would have been useful
the foot was all that could be sourced
as the lion kept the rest.

His lungs were from a local town crier who
woke a cut-throat hung-over too early in the afternoon
word has it the crier's dying wail could be heard six streets
away which beat all previous wails by a clear street

His tongue, a donation from the chairman of the
tongue twister society who could no longer
service his debts and was found face down
in the harbour though it seems the tongue
talked its way out of it eventually.

His left eye blue a wondrous thing of beauty was from
a young countess – his right eye brown her lover's
both items a generous gift from
the count himself.

His hips, a handy addition from a salty sea dog who's
run-in after falling from his ship ended kinder for the shark a
sea dog's hips, of course are self-levelling so, he glided, with
grace rather than lurched, as would be customary for a monster.

His right hand though he'd have liked it to be a fighting hand
was found on the street and was notably unskilled
its habits were unsavoury though how much of this could be
pinned on the original owner well, that's debatable.

Bird droppings in milk bottles

We found at our doorstep, bird droppings
smeared into our milk bottles. Nazi salutes
and clenched fists were expected and accepted
(but not this attempt at black humour).

They said we didn't belong here, they were right.
My father fled, dressed as an English gent,
to the land they said was flowing with milk and honey,
no one could resist the siren call.
An unnatural hunger that can't be sated,
the devil's ransom paid for the prodigal son to return
with the fatted calf (saddle full of money
to buy a Mercedes or pay for the concrete extension).
Even though I knew no other country,
I inherited his dis-belonging.

I fled too, from those who considered themselves pure. I
made a clearing in a wasteland into which I could disappear,
where I ate penny sweets (the powder white
milk bottles were my favourite) safe. And fed stale roti to
nesting chicks, they would not come at first
but I would not relent and overcame their fear.
I found some comfort in the control I had over their lives.

I couldn't hide forever, my shelter, a pyre laid to waste
returned to the soil underfoot.
Back there a double storey extension a monument to him
and the wretched work that kept him here.

His hands bloodied, the skin sliced clean off the knuckles
leaving stubs for fingers and scarred palms, by a paper press.
Rendered beyond identity, a non-person.
It would never be warm to the touch.

When I laid him down finally to rest in his Sunday best,
ran through his hair with milk and honey, I wished
I had laid my hand on his scars and forgiven,
rather than wait till all that was left were the prayers.

Girl in Black, Andalucia

Sol y sombra, mis ninas:
I leave you now, to go
the shadow way, the other way
from where you,
all you sorrowing moths
hovering now about my sinking flame,
will spill into the summer dazzle
from the dark church
of goodbyes

will dry your eyes, feel a little guilty
as you complain last year's dress
for the August Fair is too tight,
remembering
how my best black wool coat
swirled about my shrunken body

when I trembled at each step
into the early Spring sunshine;
you held me up to the warmth
as if it might revive me,
rekindle the embers

but no roaring lion sun,
no warm hands and kisses,
could keep me
from the road of the cold shadow

Broken?

If your question is am I broken
then it comes down to cracks and bricks
and the mortar or glue or bindings used
to keep those bricks together
and whether they are supposed to fit another way
or fit
at all?

If your question is am I wrong
then it comes down to both the question being asked
and who is asking
and whether the correct answer is to left or right
or whether up should rather be down
and whether being wrong on this one is better
than being right
on the next?

If your question is why me
then it comes down to you or who else
and whether it's just as well it's you and not another
and just as well for you too
that it was this why
at this time
in this way:
and why not?

The questions we ask ourselves
under the greatest weight of the nesses
of sad and lonely and tired and empty
and the ever-lurking dark
are always out of context,
flowers and freight trains both hastening in our direction
while we are looking the other way.

Hold your hand.
Make the call.
Wait.
The only certain thing

is time's obdurate refusal to play an encore
or repeat herself for long.
Stand down. Play sad music. Endure.
The voice which whispers "No one knows!"
is one of consolation
not despair.

Clever

I didn't think we knew each other well   Or so I thought
I'd pass you in the corridor, untucked, tie loosed around
your neck   not sporting affectation – cool
like the rugger boys but because they broke you always,
no point in putting yourself back together
your submission worn in a cilice of each inflicted
pull and tear and pitiful dress code violation
Too clever to be tolerated or ignored - your brilliance
a liability, awarded, *Best in Class* the biggest
prize-winning fruit at the faculty fair, all wanted to look
but none wanted to taste your flesh *too hot housed,*
too unnatural, too different for its own good
a fucking freak amongst the wholesome homegrown,
queering that much quicker where the first-place rosette
pricked you   Sometimes, to raise the tender angle
of your head I would say hello and grateful for the scrap
you'd ask, *going to Boys' Brigade?* your father,
marching you *towards true Christian manliness*
In the cold church hall, we wrapped ourselves in
Sure and Steadfast colours of our misery
You topped in Christian education, bushcraft too –
reef knot, figure eight knot, bowline, two half hitches
Too clever by half, incitement to their fingers
probing to undo and for a while, I would shun you too
that someone might make a connection – the connection
I'd watch them drilled, witchfinder's torch held high
the danger close to finding in your face as pale as wax
eyes lit by their fiery judgement – the source of you
and I would do nothing and say nothing as when your
gaze fell and lingered on the youngest sergeant there,
I did nothing and said nothing - because I knew
our misery had purpose and shared company at last
and taint by association, so I fled   your cleverness
could not save you from the burn   At your funeral
your mother said *such a good friend to him*
desperate to believe, and I wondered what knot
you'd used on the rope around your neck?
Your own brilliance finally tight around your throat

tied perfectly   hanging there inside your wardrobe,
strung from the rail of clothes so neatly pressed
I vowed to keep you close and get to know each
dazzling clever crease of you at last

Family Traits

Two photos, black and white,
sit side-by-side in my album.
In one, an old woman, clay-pipe in hand,
head tilted, arm raised to shield her eyes
from the sun, smiles towards the camera.
In the other, an old man echoes the tilt,
arm gesture and smile precisely.
They are seated on the same bench,
in front of the same shed.
Only the birch tree grown from tiny
to towering shows the years between
these photographs of my dad and his mum.
I am grateful to whoever thought
of placing them to face the sun.

Çay Bahçesi – The Tea Garden

The umber of sunset is swirling in my glass;
I stir the bitter leaves with a sugared spoon
and hope to drop down into the soil soon.

All I have craved is *this* warmth, its particular
aroma of *güller* and lost things, and the view of
an umber sunset swirling in my glass.

I'm going to dig myself in this time, a child playing
tug-of-war. I will not be moved.
I hope to drop down into the soil soon

and bury myself shallowly, so I can still hear
the *put-put* of Okay tiles playing endlessly,
and the sugar sunset dissolving in my glass.

Brassy clouds and sweet peas. If you please,
I have settled my bill already, am I free to go
spooning myself gently into the soil soon?

I have eaten midday and the afternoon
in the softness of this seat's caress.
While the umber of sunset is swirling in my glass,
let me seed myself sweetly in the soil, and bloom.

Nothing Ground-Breaking

Just the newt who poked its head out of the net
curiously, before it slipped away. Or the peonies,
arranging themselves carefully into a spring
bouquet. Sometimes the footfall on the street
at night, dark figures talking softly, not wanting
to wake the neighbours with their secrets.
Rain, magnificent, tiny rain. Reminding the skin
what it means to be touched, to be chosen
as a landing place. Lost things placed on fence
posts and rubbish bins; passers-by hoping for
a reunion. Sunlight resting in surprising places:
the top of the treehouse, the spine of a book,
your hands. A greenfly navigating your fingers;
your palms turned upwards to receive nothing
ground-breaking. You, blossoming, feet to
fingertips, opening up for the world, drinking
in a breeze that can't be captured.

Threnody: On the Death of Lorca

I listen to fence wattles applauding the light
and the tympanic rattle of green shutters
followed by a descant of geraniums. I hear notes
wrung from their red hearts, the *siguirillas* of the South.

Yes, this is the place. Here a polyphonic river runs over
stones, makes pools for horses to dip heads and drink.
Can you hear whispered confessions at the water's edge
where the priest's voice is the cry of a heron?

And women's whispers, rising from brown birds pecking
at leaves under trees? Someone sings a sad ballad
in the shade of an olive tree, it's an old story, asking
to be planted beneath the vine-roots when love dies;

like on that night when stars were strung together with songs
before the sun came up and burned away all smiles.

*Federico Garcia Lorca, gay poet and playwright, executed
in August 1939 by Nationalists during the Spanish Civil War.*

Oiling the Chain

My son cycles from Skipton to Skelton.
I've made it, he beeps. Maybe
it's my wishes that turn his wheels:

I never learnt, you see -
my mother said there wouldn't be bicycles
by the time I grew up, so what's the point?

I borrowed Lindy's sister's bike, several sizes bigger
than my skill, and persistently fell off
in the face of oncoming traffic. On balance,

it's perhaps as well I stopped.
There's still a hand-me-down thrill,
to think of my flesh and blooded knees

whooshing along a genetic tightrope
not of my making, making it
all the way to Skelton, almost making up

for some sort of missing link
in the family history of going places.

Synaesthete

I'm trying to understand:
new school, cool art teacher.
Sargent's Lady Macbeth,
her barbed jagged gown,
the command to discuss
what we see...But her dress stabs
my eyes, its belts drag me into a bloody
hell, the raised crown breathes
pungent lilies. One of her braids sneaks
snake-like into my mouth, burns
my throat, flashes a sparked circuit.
I gag. My gut's a carousel.
The painting shatters.
Glass screams across the studio floor
streams off
to highlands and heaths, tumbles
in the slime of warrior stench.
I throw up. Splatter shoes, table legs,
someone's art: orchestras, kaleidoscopes,
bent-tin yelps and eyeball blame.
Everything's orange. Shock's always orange.

Ethan Myers laughs. Stupid bitch,
he says, so I deck him, hard, my fist
a tangle of entrails, his cheek a billowy
sponge. On impact, out dance a rosy
row of thumbs-up leprechauns.
Ethan's bellow's a wounded
elephant, he clutches his grey face.

And now comes that bladed
silence: The End of the World.
Cool Teacher takes
me to an edgeless, endless room,
bubbles Disney words, twirls rags
of marshmallow calm, waits
for my swollen senses to settle,
releases me back into the wild.

Ghost Town

One blast from a bass saxophone,
A solo foghorn loud enough
To send a shiver down the spine of the sleeping heavens.
No response.

Under the waves one desperate whale fires off
A machine gun rattle of 'click clicks'
Desperate to find the others
Abandoned by the pod.
No response.

On the edge of the sea
where the town meets the hem of the tide,
Rusted skeletal cranes, heads bowed down
As if deep in prayer at their own funeral.
Around the town, the shuffling of feet.
People like gamblers who've been
Dealt a losing hand of cards.

Before there had been promises
Gift-wrapped in a cacophony of hope,
Now all silenced.
The last lighthouse reduced to rubble,
Final beacon already disappeared into the shadows
Now a dark shroud wrapping the seas.
On land, their futures pickpocketed, the people cheated
Tears swell like broken tides
In the ghost town.

No zig-zagging ferries
Merely a forlorn straight line across the bay.
Beneath the waves
The whale repeats itself in circles.
And so it plans its escape
Accepts its fate
Better to be stranded
Than abandoned like
A single star in the night sky.

In the town, the sarcastic cackle of the herring gulls
As they nip the heels of the discarded.

Walking with Aristotle along Aberdeen beach

To tighten up his logic and his dialectic
Aristotle perambulated Greece; en route he refined
his killer arguments and insights that reverberate
even to a super-clever, taut, post-modern mind:

his thesis, antithesis and synthesis
have shaped philosophy, whilst the light he shined
on ethics illuminates life still. His acolytes
formed the Peripatetic School, and today I find

myself in parallel guise, tuning lines for poetry:
avoiding the main drag of Union Street, I take Back Wynd
to reach the unsung sands of Aberdeen:
no pre-determined pathways here, ideas roam unconfined;

a sharp Easterly blasts brain-fluff with the spume
and lifts me up as if I fly, and I am disinclined to disagree
with anyone on anything. Philosophy, though, interrupts:
Does escape like this devalue effort in the daily grind?

Do love, dreams, art, make work seem worthless?
No, not to me. Contrarily, they more remind
me of the separate remit and reward of labour:
devoting energy to business, being paid, both much-maligned

as though they are somehow inferior to 'me time',
or lacking 'higher aims' in a universe designed
by Allah, God, or Brahma, that we subserve.
Surveying this Sunday morningscape, what I've divined

is less the consequence of deity than human happenstance:
strangers to me stroll in tandem, hands and arms combined,
sharing children, dogs, each other, conversating lives, as I,
I too, walk the beach, adrift in time, poetry and purpose
realigned.

The Dandelion Clock

The soul is in the body
as light is in the air, Plotinus thought.
Light being God's factotum --
Light, and air,
and time, so restless, setting off
soft detonations
of the dandelion clocks,
the thistle globes.
Every flight
is a crossing over,
a controlled fall,
setting seed. Seeing this,
it's no wonder we bristle and rush.
Small wonder, we deny.
Time is forever managing our damage
into finitudes. Sending
all our briefs and declamations
rattling down the stairwell.
In time, though not quite yet
we may become
transparent with the joy of this,
carried over,
lifting off.

April Blooms With Red
In memory of Iryna

Your hand does not belong here
In this muddy ground
Pale skin yet to merge with the grey matter
The redness yet to fade
And still contrasting with the lifeless earth
You painted your nails with so much care,
So much affection
All the tiny details planned out exactly
And rendered with piety
And the smile on your face when you did it

In March you saw the colours for the last time
You could raise your fingers subtly
To watch the red glimmering in pale sunlight
Barely lurking from behind the grey sky with
Smoke travelling high into the clouds
The air was brisk, the ground cold and lifeless
The city falling asleep to the sound of killing
Before the night even came
The glimmer of red growing to become the sea

You did not belong there
Your hands should be moving
Fingers warm with blood circulating in them
But it was in April that I saw them for the last time
Pale but covered with the most vibrant colour
The only colour standing out from the ashen ground

An Order

What is an order?
If I spell it with a capital O
it's a fraternity or a sorority, that's a group,
of monks or nuns
mostly in silent contemplation,
navels exposed, metaphorically speaking,
and they still communicate as and when,
and the guy or woman,
the chief monk or nun,
the abbot or mother superior,
lip read and signs, and God bless
any of them who mouth obscenities
for he, or she, will damn you with lip speak and froth
and make the sign of the cross
and point you out
as if giving an order.
Is that why they are called an Order?
Benedictines, Carthusians, Trappists,
you and me if we keep our traps shut,
our carts after the horses,
and our benedictions out of sight.
Last orders, please.
But are all the other ones in the right order?
Buddhists, I forgot Buddhists.
They are the order of the day,
can clap with one hand,
use a capital O
when the chant, Oum.
Can I take your order?
I'll have a Bud, please,
and a new mantra.

House of Thorns
(After a sculpture by Alice Maher)

Each spike was a sharp
protesting tongue
in a family where everyone
had the last word.

I swallowed it down whole
though it was painful
and now it galls inside–
rectangular porcupine.

Each thorn was grown with care:
if you lifted the roof
would you find a rosebud
plush petals, shades of red?

More likely a swarm
of stinging rebukes
buzzing with self righteousness–
no honeyed words.

What did the neighbours think,
in their terraced, homely way,
to have a problem family:
always shouting, slamming doors?

I know we guarded ourselves well,
all the thorns pointed outwards
so no Prince could wake us
with a tender word.

Our clanging squabbles echoed
back and forth until the house
wore crowns of black spikes,
hostile walls, refusing change.

The Writer Abroad

You would have known his tousled elegance
as I did, from back-cover photos. Older,
with a sag of one cheek, but unmistakeable.
'A long friendship,' I told them at the funeral
but the sum was that chance afternoon
sitting out by the chug and echo of a lesser canal.
Thirty years had marinated his voice in wine,
peppered his English with Venetian obscenities.

Idle during the floods, he messaged me,
warm, witty and unwise, a new Decameron
in his tales of desirous lovers in dank *palazzi*.
His chat blazed with an inner-circle brilliance,
a spinning top of names. Bidding to rival him,
I revved up the cleverness in my replies. *Con amore*,
signing off as he had. His irony, my sincerity.
No answer. Was I too eager, a minor character?

He died a half-year on. Three wailing ex-lovers
and a mezzo singing of unappeasable grief.
A Nobel poet, the consul, London editors, all
went off to a bar in St Mark's, beginning to talk
of other business

He lies easy on purple velvet,
the Times obituary spread across his chest
until the wind takes it. It is just another story
taking flight, perhaps not told quite as he'd have wished.
His face expresses no alarm.
I am the underpaid gondolier
who ferries him across a void to the Isle of the Past.

To The Other Side: (Wheeled and Drenched)

for my grandpa who fled from China in 1949

To the other side: wheeled and drenched
                    ships rolled
                              sparse: away
          thunder knotted in the woods
    lumps of salt, ropes and all: loosen
                         ice quaked
        reckless   piece of frozen soil   deck
                           rang through   bells
    stones   the daughter   born *over there: whimpered*

                    *

          Laid low / heaviness / journey
    unrelinquished, head of wrung rippling
              wild flowers, heads –
    edged a little / stirred / but soon drew distant
    far from every: evening star / her tiny toes / country dog:
                                        bark
        wrapped, cotton soaked, on ridge of dazzling dune
                    falling   snow, cushioned
                         slide back slide   back
        to hollow strait, cool-vessel: bones *strewed*
                                        on and on
                ran deep – shadowy   lighthouse
                    cyan dream / dissolved
                an egg: *clashed*, oval, hand palms
                         pumping over
                dawn-veined
    began to take shape and flow: *dimpled*
                              in silence

November was a month

November was a month of deep-breath skies,
glowering and biblical,
a month of hunched hillsides and flooded fields.
November was a month of weak blue skies,
of expressive trees and staunch birds.
November was a month of rainbows.

November was a month of trees treacled with colour,
a month miserly with her sunshine,
of dark hedgerows and roads awash,
and of rainbows.

And those rainbows! Those rainbows
were rich and arcing and sweetshop bright,
they straddled horizons,
they diminuted everything below them –
they made a pencil of a cathedral spire!

Those November rainbows
reduced to a captive
each tense, folded landscape
made wakeful
to stare-gazey upwards
as seeming silent spectators
cowed, and awed and utterly floored.

November was the month of rainbows,
of poetry come to life.
You should have been there
during November,
the month that was
the month of rainbows.

Artist with a Scalpel
after Bonjour Professor Calne, John Bellany

I turn his hands over in mine
his yellowed palms flushed pink
with toxins from his failing liver.
Oil paint has seeped into the creases,
stained cuticles etched in charcoal.
His abdomen is my canvas.

I press the tip of my scalpel blade,
make the first bold clean incision
watch beads of crimson ooze coalesce
in a line, a pout of fat opens beneath
as I cauterise through silvered fascia,

muscle fibres, pearlescent peritoneum
lifting it between the splayed web
of my gloved fingers, to protect organs
beneath, explore his abdominal cavity's
secrets with the crook of my fingers.

As soon as he comes round he needs
drawing paper to prove he is alive,
calls his pencils analgesics.
Now his paintings blaze with colour.

The poets

TJ (Tim) Armstrong is the prize-winning author of *Walter and the Resurrection of G* and *Cecilia's Vision*. He has also worked as an educator, linguist, translator and musician. He lives in Canterbury, Kent.

Alice Brooker is an undergraduate studying History and English at the University of Oxford. This is her first poem in a print publication; more of her work can be found online at the Young Poets Network. Her hobbies include baking, long walks and reading too much romantic fiction.

Pete Concahsmith lives in Somerset with his wife, three-year-old son and dog. He likes to renovate houses. He is a keen potter, has been a poet since the age eight, and is thrilled to be included.

Bal Dhillon has an MA in Screenwriting from the University of the Arts, London. He wrote the poem in this anthology in memory of his late father. Bal lives in London with his three kids and combines writing with work as a lawyer.

Francesca Duffield is a writer and artist originally from the Midlands now living in Lewes, East Sussex. She has worked as an illustrator and art lecturer, and taught English as a Second Language. She has had poems included in anthologies by Bourne to Write and published in *Ingenue* magazine.

Steven Duggan is a poet, novelist and short-story writer living on the east coast of Ireland. His work has appeared in publications including *Poetry*, *Rattle*, *Savoy Magazine*, *Planet Ireland* and *The Edgeworth Papers*. His first collection of poems, *Fully Formed*, placed second for the 2022 Patrick Kavanagh Poetry Award.

Derek Ferguson was born in Dundee, brought up in Troon, living in London. He has done a bit of everything, everywhere – art galleries; drugs charities; photography archives, liberating images from the dusty depths of windowless warehouses. He's now attempting the same with words.

Max Fishel was born at a very early age in Liverpool, and now resides London. European Jewish ancestry. Plays Irish music, writes poems, worries about hair loss. Mainly analogue, partly digital. Has been published a bit. Loves performing at spoken word open mic events. Owns a couple of nice jackets.

Eileen Anne Gordon lives in Bath. She grew up in Scotland and has lived in England, Ireland and Finland. She started writing poetry after retirement and has been published in magazines and anthologies. Apart from her grandchildren, poetry and gardening are her old-age energisers.

Yasmin Inkersole is a British-Turkish poet from Oxfordshire, with an MA in Creative Writing. She writes about Turkish culture, heritage and migration among other topics. Yasmin's debut pamphlet, *Selene*, won the Hedgehog Press First Pamphlet Competition and will be published in 2024.

Pam Job lives in Essex. Her poems are widely anthologised.

Sue Kindon lives and writes in the French Pyrenees. She was runner-up in the 2021 Ginkgo Prize (for eco-poetry); her latest pamphlet is *Outside, the Box* (4Word Press, 2019). She sometimes writes in French.

Lizzi Linklater writes poetry, fiction and scripts; lectures; runs writing and literary events. She is published in *Dream Catcher*, *Circa Works*, *YorkMix*, *Lives Remembered* (The York Press). She has poetry set to music with the Sounds Lyrical Project. In 2022 she compiled and published the anthology *Something Brewing* (Lendal Press/Valley Press).

Frank Lowry was born in Birkenhead, Merseyside. For 32 years he taught History in a comprehensive school in a socially-deprived area. His passions are anything to do with the natural world and literature especially poetry.

Charlie Mawer works as a creative director in advertising. Bafta-nominated for National Poetry Day design, he was published in publications including *Poetry Now London*, *Envoi* and *Poetry South*, and won a Tennyson Prize, judged by Michael Rosen, before a long hiatus to have kids. He now publishes a poem a day.

Mike Mackillop-Hall won first prize aged 12 reading Masefield's 'I must go down to the seas again...' in school Eisteddfod. He started writing at 16 and worked for 35 years, with intermittent poems. Now he loves writing poetry, thanks to Oxford ContEd Workshops, all the time.

Lawrence McDowell is a married father of two from Edinburgh. He has a job in the public sector and spends his working days looking at screens, numbers and data. In real life he enjoys ancient history, poetry and being outdoors.

Katarzyna Piecuch is an English graduate currently studying English literature and literary criticism in Poland. She is a Virginia Woolf enthusiast, poetry and vintage fashion lover and an avid coffee drinker who enjoys travelling, skiing, art in all its shapes, cinematography and rock and indie music.

Jennifer M Phillips is a bi-national immigrant, painter, gardener, Bonsai-grower. Her chapbooks are *Sitting Safe In the Theatre of Electricity* (i-blurb.com, 2020) and *A Song of Ascents* (Orchard Street Press, 2022). A poem is like a little brass pan to carry fire's coals through the winter, and so she writes.

Anthony Powers previously worked as a doctor in general practice and has been a writer for 12 years, holding a BA (Hons) in English Literature and Creative Writing. He has had several poems published in magazines and anthologies.

Martin Rieser was 2021 winner of the Hastings Poetry Competition, runner-up for Norman Nicnolson 2020, short-listed in Frosted Fire 2019 /2022; Charles Causeley Prize 2020; Wolves Poetry Competition 2022. Longlisted for the Erbecce Prize 2023. His poems have been widely published.

Derek Sellen has written poetry, stories and plays over many years. He has read his work in the UK and Europe and won various awards, including Poets Meet Politics, O'Bheal Five Words and the Canterbury Festival. His collection *The Other Guernica* was a finalist in the Poetry Book Award 2020.

Shi-Min Sun was born in 1993 in Taipei, Taiwan. She started writing while working abroad, inspired by family and friends. She received an award of merit from the Atlanta Review 2022 International Poetry Competition, and has been published in *Assignment* literary magazine, *The Broadkill Review, The Wild Word*, and *The New Verse News*.

Sally Stanford lives in South West France surrounded by Cognac vines which are a constant inspiration for her poetry. Apart from her focus on poems she has recently been writing creative non-fiction. She has a degree in Art History; countless paintings have evoked imagery and ideas for her work.

Steve Stevenson was born and raised in the UK's Peak District. He's spent his working life as a documentary film editor. About five years ago, he made his first forays into poetry, the composition of which is in many ways analogous to editing film, but without the constraints of budget, schedule and broadcast.

Marcus Tickner took a leap out of teaching and into writing. Combined with daily school runs and renovating his house, this offered him an opportunity to write poetry for adults and children that he hopes to publish. He lives with his beautiful, ever-supportive partner, Jodie, and their two children, Anna and Edward.

Christian Ward is a UK-based writer who has recently appeared in *Rappahannock Review, South Florida Poetry Journal, The Dewdrop, Dodging the Rain, Wild Greens, Mad Swirl*, Dipity literary magazine, *Impspired*, and *Streetcake* magazine. His first collection, *Intermission*, is out now.

Judith Wozniak has an MA in Writing Poetry. Her poems have appeared in *The Alchemy Spoon, Fenland Poetry Journal, The Frogmore Papers, London Grip* and *Ink Sweat & Tears*. She won first prize in the Hippocrates Competition 2020. Her pamphlet, *Patient Watching*, was published by The Hedgehog Press in 2022.

About the cover illustrator

René Shoemaker is a master silk painter, born in New York City, who maintains studios in Athens, GA, USA and Aubusson, France. Spanning four decades and embracing a variety of media, her artwork highlights a sense of place while capturing the ways spaces work together and how people inhabit and interact with those spaces. René has exhibited in museums in Georgia, Mississippi, and Paris and in galleries and public spaces in Georgia, New York, the UK, and France. She teaches and speaks on silk painting and in 2020 she received a Forward Focus Fellowship from AIR Serenbe in Georgia.

www.reneshoemaker.com

Photo © Jean-Marc Gargantiel
jmgargantiel.zenfolio.com

Artemesia Arts...

...was formed in 2022 for poets and writers to celebrate literature and poetry in the English language. As a charitable association, Artemesia Arts exists to encourage writing and to support writers, both aspirational and professional, in their creative craft. The association holds an annual poetry festival in the medieval village of Treignac in south-west France.

This year Artemesia Arts launched its international poetry competition and this anthology includes the winners, runners-up and an eclectic selection of the most compelling poems submitted. All poems were chosen by the competition judges, the well-known poet, playwright, broadcaster and children's author Roger McGough, and Sheila Schofield, who co-founded Artemesia Arts with the poet Kate Rose.

Artemesia Arts recognizes the value of creative writing in advancing well-being and cultural diversity. The association is looking ahead to a bright future promoting good writing and encouraging cultural collaboration in France, Europe and beyond.

www.artemesia-arts.com